# My Nostalgia Colour Palette

Hazel Carino

BookLeaf Publishing

India | USA | UK

Presentation by *BookLeaf Publishing*

Web: www.bookleafpub.com

E-mail: info@bookleafpub.com

ISBN: 9789358318456

First edition 2023

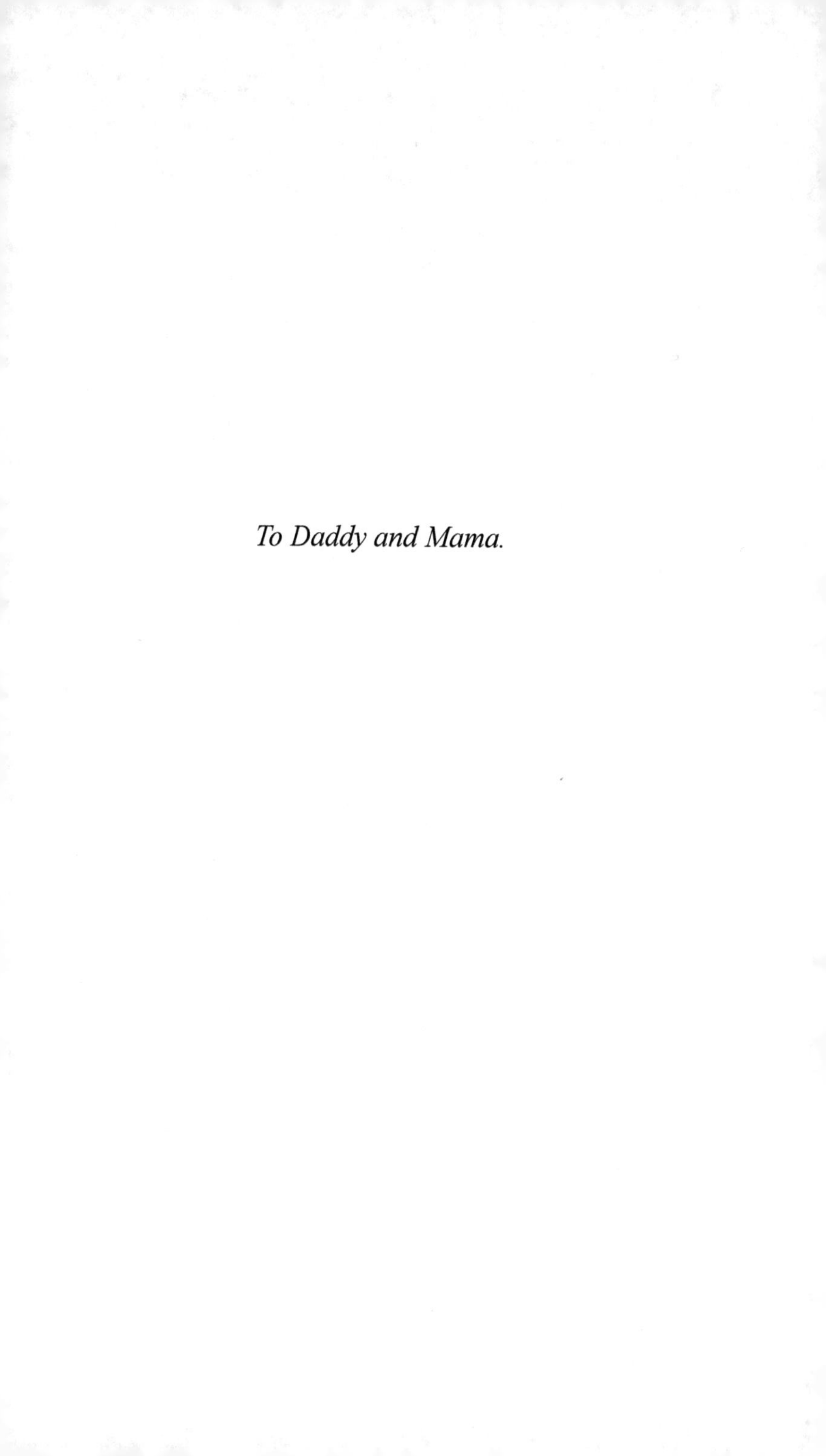

*To Daddy and Mama.*

# ACKNOWLEDGEMENT

To my friends and family, wherever in the world
you may be.

# PREFACE

My memories are not just black and white.

They are colourful.

# White as a canvass

Today was white
blank as a canvass
the road ahead was unclear
I needed a compass

This page was blank
like the sky when it's making a decision
whether to let the sun out or rain down my
frustrations

This page was white and pure like a bride
a new month begins,
to silence the sadness I hide
I drew the curtains to let in the sunlight

Like when I first arrived
the walls were white
they took me in and reflected back
all that was inside

The walls are white and I've been staring at it
for hours
It's been years, I'm a big girl now
I think I'll just cry in the shower

# Pink like my mother

Some days are pink like
flowers for my mother
on the day they honour the dead back home
like candles on my table
the scent feels like her embrace

Some days are pink
like my lips on a Wednesday
when I pretend I'm not cold
I'm still a child
This sadness I can't outgrow

Some days are pink just like my mother
at least I remember that is what they used to call
her
I wore the pink and I chose the flowers
home becomes my memories of
 her scent that still lingers

# Purple is my favourite dessert

If purple was edible I think it would be sweet
It would taste like the rice cakes my
grandmother used to make

If purple was edible I'd have it for breakfast
everyday
So I can taste home again and fill up this empty
space

If purple was on the menu I'd order it every time
It might fill up this hunger
Or consume the monsters I hide

If purple was the third course
I'll never be too full
I'll always have room for dessert, I would finish
it all

# Orange, you glad you didn't marry me?

Orange was the sky that day
When I rushed home to cry behind the door
after I learned you were not going to stay

Orange were the leaves that touched me on the
cheeks
As they fall from the trees
When I walked past crying in discreet

Orange was the taste of an entire year
because everything was sour
except the salty tears

Orange were the dreams that haunt me on nights
for I'll never be the bride
And I keep losing my grip even if I hold tight

Orange is the sky in my memory
and I'm a fast strong girl running at the sunset
on the day that I learned you'll never marry me

# Green eyed monster in my mirror selfie

There's a green eyed monster in my mirror selfie
Her face looks young
but she's full of apathy

There's a green eyed monster in my mirror selfie
Her stomach is flat
but she's jealous of your new family

There's a green eyed monster in my mirror selfie
Her arms are toned
but she's tired of what she carries

There's a green eyed monster in my mirror selfie
Her hair is shiny
but her head is in a frenzy

There's a green eyed monster in my mirror selfie
Her outfit is on fleek
but she's lost her identity

# The buses are red but the phone booths don't work

Everyone rush to catch the train or bus
No one really stops to look at the sky
Except when it rains
Umbrellas up high

Days just go by without seeing the light
sun and stars are just passersby
except when the trains are delayed
We stop for awhile to let out a sigh

Tourists just come and go like the tide
Waves of faces that never go dry
Strangers before then strangers again
Friends and lovers just pass you by

In a portrait of grey red is the bus
but those phone booths don't work
and we are disconnected
In the city of irony for people like us

# Azure Manila Sky

I miss the azure Manila sky
and the soup we liked in Chinatown
I miss the taste of Ube ice cream
and maddening rush when the rain pours down

I miss the ice cold beer
and the seafood plates
I miss the rock band venue
you were so drunk you couldn't walk straight

I miss the sunset in Manila bay
and how I never used to pay attention
I miss leaning on the bus window to cry
and hide all my frustrations

I miss the smell of grilled street food
and the overcrowded train
I miss the sound of karaoke
to drown the sound of pain

I miss the scorching summer heat
and the things we used to do
I even miss the smoke and rain
but I don't think I still miss you

# Blood on my blue scrubs

There's blood on my blue scrubs but it isn't
mine
It's your mother's or brother's
but they'll be just fine


There are drops on my blue crocs
but surgery's done
The stats are ok
and your husband can walk

There is sweat on my pink hat
but I can exhale
We are closing the skin now
we've given all that we got

There's dirt on my white gloves
but the lump is all gone
doctor has given his all
and we've replaced his blood

There's hunger in my belly
but it's worth all these hours
some people are better and
I am full with the triumph of surgery

# Mahogany

If mahogany had a scent,
It's the smell of old books
and my fathers thinking face
and his concerned look

If mahogany was a story
I think I've read it all
My father showed me the edition
of a book by the shelf mounted on the wall

If mahogany was a problem
I think I could find the solution
He already showed me the way
It is clear with an explanation

If mahogany was a scent
It would be on top of my list
the books I read are my father's treasure
I have inherited this bliss

# Running into the crimson

It takes a while to start
and then I catch my air
At first it feels like flying
Except your wings are bare

I accelerate as I feel the ground
separate from under my feet
I can feel my breathing
And the thunder in my heartbeat

I turn the bend and I feel the pavement
I begin to clear my head
My heels in a rhythm
In the reddish sunset, my hunger has been fed

And then it hits me as I look at the horizon
That I don't know where I'm going
I am aimless, I just want to be free
So I run as fast as I can into the crimson

# Yellow way out

I've been walking around in circles
Looking for the yellow way out
been up and down staircases
full of anxiety and self doubt

I've been travelling to nowhere
Always trying to catch a train
Living and always trying to get there
waiting to numb the pain

I've been up and down this station
but I don't know where to go
I've never known for years of hesitation
where this sea of crowds flow

I've been trying and hoping to move on
but I'm stuck in a moment of my fears
I've been dreaming of being done
Been trying to shift gears

I've been walking round in circles
Looking for the yellow way out
of my fears and hesitation
out of all of my self doubt

# Red dress made of red flags

I made a red dress out of your red flags and I'm
wearing it with this hat
I put some sequins from the tears you've caused
me and the zip from
keeping my mouth shut


I made a red dress with your red flags
and I'm showing off in town
how it fits every curve and corner of the fabric
made of fooling around


There's now a red dress from your red flags and
it hangs proudly in my closet
It whispers many warnings
and the ruffles are made of regret


I made a red dress from your red flags, and my
friends, they envy me
It hangs closely to body
and it squeezes my lungs
of air and sensibility

# Between gravel and grey skies

I am a silhouette, waking back and forth in the
cold darkness
The sun never really shines here
I am a being, travelling these lonely roads
I don't know what is coming near

I am a force and I don't know which one is
morning
I don't see the light in this endless
tunnel
I am a waste of sanity in this light forbidden
place

I am a traveller in a long and cold winter
In between gravel and grey skies
I don't know who I am
I don't know who I have become

I used to be water but now I'm nothing but ice
I surrender my radiance to the cold wind
I am tired and I have not seen light
I am silent, I am crumbling in between gravel
and grey skies

# Silver bolts

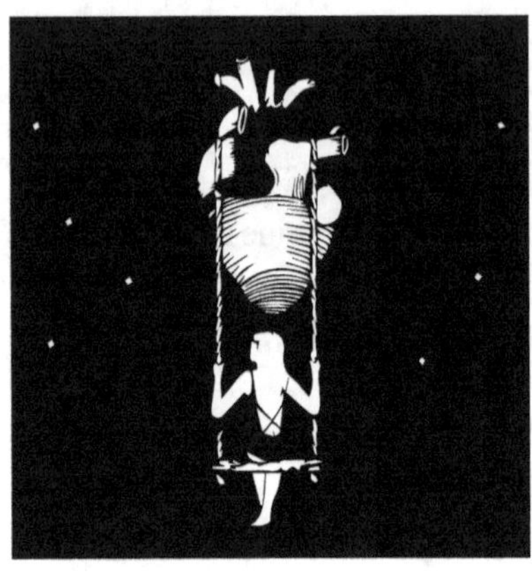

I tie myself into a figure of eight
to make sure my hope is intact
I tighten my harness and squeeze all the air of
hesitation from my mind and from my stomach

I clip myself into the first bolt and hang into my
first triumph
I carried on until I'm halfway through and the
anchor is no longer as high up

I ask to take so I can release my arms and all my
building frustrations
I push my fingers into the cracks
and breathe out my fear and desperation

Despite bleeding fingers and taped up hope
I call my alter ego to keep on climbing
I clipped the top bolt,  it's cold and silver and in
the sunlight it is shining

# Black and blue

I train for days and even weeks
I place my fears into a glass jar
I hit the bag with my closed fist
and throw my worries to somewhere far

I wrap my hands and uncover my rage
I tape my gloves to secure my fate
I guard my mouth as I step the stage
but I bear my heart and it's shattered state

I take the punch, I take each blow
I move my feet back and around
I put Vaseline and I let go
to the hollow where the punch is the only sound

I'm black and blue but I am whole
I've been hurt worse before
I choose the ropes cause they keep me safe
and I feel my fist explode when the crowd roars

# My dreams of home are pale yellow and smell of Mangoes

A shelf of brown books, a bowl of mangoes and
me running endlessly into a hallway
I'm chasing the memories that are fading gently
into the pages of old books

My father's old books
My untuned guitar and the violin covered in
cobwebs by the corner
and playing melodies that are never finished

My old harmonica and my butterfly knife
and the slingshot I kept in the box
My mother's old plates
My grandmother's hot chocolate that I never
stopped to crave

The browning teen band posters
The dusty rag dolls
and the sunset that always shines through the
mango trees

My dreams of home are pale yellow
and I chase them in my English bed
they smell of mangoes and old books
and they feel of a warmth I will never feel again

# Red wine and longing

I watch it flow to my empty glass
like gushing blood, I have seen this before
I smell the hint of bold regret
and  I see the tint of longing

I swirl it around like my chaotic thoughts
so the flavour wraps all of me
the smell of alcohol begins
and red is now the colour of my anxiety

I drink some more to warm my soul
that I don't know is still there
these glacial nights, they have no cure
and my anticipation is lost somewhere

The room begins to blur again
the lights begin to shimmer
It's red it's gushing into my arteries
drowning my longing with a drop and a glimmer

# Rainy days are porpoise grey

I don't like the feel of rainy Tuesdays and when
it's porpoise grey
The city wants me out of my bed
but my dreams are multi coloured


I don't like the chill that stings me
and the way my wet hoodie clings
into my face and my motivation


I don't feel the feet under my socks
and my hands under my coat's pockets
I'm just a hollow fragment under this waterproof
jacket


I don't see against the mist and blinding
headlights
I chase the time as I cross the street
but the street is wet and uninviting, icy and just
sleet

Rainy days are porpoise grey and my heart is
void of sunshine
Even rainbows don't come through if they have
invites from the colourblind

# Magenta Lips

Is it the shade of my lip tint
that makes you think I'm weak?
Didn't you take the hint
when I began to speak?

You thought I couldn't outrun you
or I cannot throw a punch or two
You think I couldn't climb higher
Think I can't do more press ups than you

You think I couldn't do better
than that male one
You think I could not hold for longer
You think shortly I'll be done

You talk to me like I'm stupid
you treat me like I'm unfit
you assume I cannot do it
Is it my magenta lips?

# Red door

There is a red door which I've kept hidden
into the depths of my memory
behind it is a lot of clutter
from years of relentless controversy

There is a red door which I have forgotten
and erased into my apathy
inside it are the times of turmoil
and untamed anxiety

There is a red door between us
In between my forgetfulness
It is blocking all my chaos
and my well deserved rest

There is a red door that separates me from all
my rage and melancholy
It is shielding me from my anger
and the force of my hidden realities

# Chartreuse

We met at the end of summer
when the trees are all chartreuse
when the leaves are slowly giving up
and the sunsets seem confused

I first saw you just before autumn
when the leaves are still hesitant
and I was slowly losing hope
like euphoria was too distant

I felt you at the edge of summer
just before the cold wind blows
just before I fade into the darkness
and disappear where the silence goes

You touched me just before the fall
just before the leaves let go
just before my lips dry up
just before I get wrapped in shadows

You held me just before I crumbled
just before I drifted into the blues
just by the end of summer
when everything was painted chartreuse

www.ingramcontent.com/pod-product-compliance
Lightning Source LLC
La Vergne TN
LVHW010951200726
843509LV00013B/2372